# Universal Radiance

## Illuminating the Sayings of Jesus of Nazareth

J Matthews

Copyright © J Matthews

# Contents

# Introduction

*"And as they departed, Jesus began to say unto the multitudes concerning John, What went ye out into the wilderness to see? A reed shaken with the wind?"*

Matthew 11:7 King James Version

I was raised Christian and the church got my attention early. When I was seven, I contracted a virus which kept me out of school for two weeks. Though I managed to stay out of the hospital, I wasn't doing well. I remember the nausea, the fatigue, and the fear – being sick is a fearful thing, especially for a child.

After days of feverish torment, I suddenly felt well. Not "better," but completely, joyfully well. I jumped off the sofa - where a moment before I'd lain moaning - and danced around the living room, demanding solid food instead of the soup broth I'd been sipping for days.

My mother and sister came back from a walk and asked me if I was feeling better. *Better?* I was transformed.

My mother told me they'd walked to Saint Peter's church (the church we attended in our town in Vermont) and lit a candle for me. We determined I was healed in that instant.

Coincidence? If so, it was a miraculous coincidence. I've never experienced anything like it since.

When it comes to religious study, I bought the whole package. I studied theology at the Catholic University of Louvain. Then, I attended the Episcopal Divinity School of Cambridge.

After divinity school, I studied Tibetan Buddhism seriously, even living and practicing with Buddhist nuns. I also studied Advaita Vedanta – a form of inquiry based on the ancient philosophical writings of India.

Spiritual experiences, deep meditations and wakeful nights convinced me of a truth I somehow knew already: only God (or Love) is real, and all else is an innocent play of divine manifestation, like the iridescence on a soap bubble's surface.

We feel like we're separate from God and on a journey, alone. But we're never separate from God and we are certainly never alone.

After graduating from divinity school, I worked in a homeless shelter; a common path for non-ordination track divinity students who want to do good. I had an insight about the Christian path one morning, while running a support group for adults in our substance use program.

The program participants were there for substance use treatment, but that morning they wanted to talk about the ridiculous clothing donations the shelter received. They weren't wrong (white sneakers and black socks!) but they were a little obsessed with organizing clothing drives for homeless adults that would include more fashionable items.

As a counselor, I knew these folks were experiencing *resistance*: the tug-of-war we feel when we want to change, but we don't want to change. Specifically, they were struggling with the understandable but premature desire to return to self-sufficiency.

It's hard to accept support as an adult. Adults often express resistance by trying to improve the treatment environment instead of allowing themselves to be nurtured by it.

The essential strategy for dealing with resistance is just to roll with it. When that doesn't work, one can gently point it out. I was too outnumbered to roll with the resistance, so I decided to point it out. With a lame attempt at humor, I said:

"Is this why you all came here? To see the glamorous fashion in the homeless shelters of Boston?"

Suddenly, it hit me. I'd heard this before.

*But what went ye out for to see? A man clothed in soft raiment? behold, they that wear soft clothing are in kings' houses.*

Matthew 11:8, King James Version.

If you were raised in the Christian tradition, you'll know the sayings of Jesus are generally interpreted allegorically, to reveal something about His divine origin, His relationship with humanity, or the coming Kingdom of God. I'd read them that way, too. But this saying suddenly seemed straightforward, conversational. I realized it was a rhetorical device to focus the crowd on their original intention.

The people around John the Baptist were probably organizing a clothing drive for John, who was famously unfashionable. And they were doubtless scheming to get better food than locusts and honey.

Their original intention was to find peace of mind and feel cherished by God. We are always with God, but from time to time the thought occurs that we don't deserve God's infinite love. So, we go on futile journeys to prove ourselves.

Meanwhile, God's infinite love immediately transforms our desert worlds into therapy centers to teach us that only love is real.

We insist on seeing things otherwise. We think everything is broken and we're in charge of fixing it.

Once we look beyond our feelings of guilt, we can see that only love is real. Jesus calls this ever-present realm of peace and love the Kingdom of God.

Instead of reading the sayings of Jesus as allegory, I started reading them as advice from a spiritual friend. I'd like to share the results of my new way of reading with you. I've put some of these sayings and parables in a modern context for ease of interpretation.

# 1. The Kingdom of God

*(T)he kingdom of God is within you.*

Luke 17:21, King James Version

Spiritual teachers exude love and peace because they've immersed themselves in love and peace.

Do you learn French by ignoring the French language and avoiding French people?

No, you learn French by immersion.

Love and peace are known through familiarity - they are not discovered by thinking.

If you want love and peace, seek them directly in your heart.

Don't wait to return to love until you've puzzled something out.

Let yourself dissolve into the love that you are in the very center of your heart, and everything will fall into place.

I could tell you the Kingdom is all around you until I'm blue in the face, but clearly you seek the Kingdom because you don't see it. You only see and feel "your life."

Try not to read these words to make your life better. You don't yet know what your life is.

If you let these words touch your heart, a thousand gardens of heaven will bloom this instant.

So, if you have even one good ear, please try to listen.

# 2. The Light of God

*Neither do men light a candle, and put it under a bushel, but on a candlestick; and it giveth light unto all that are in the house.*

Matthew 5:15, King James Version

You are the Light of God; you are the Universal Radiance.

For the moment, it seems you've chosen not to lavish yourself on all things.

Maybe you think you're saving your Love Light for your family and friends. But you don't seem to be lavishing love on them, either.

What are you doing? It's like you lit a candle and put it in the closet.

Love expands forever, and its only function is to be given freely. So, let your Love Light shine.

You won't save your oil by putting it out. Yours is a magic lamp – it grows ever brighter by shining.

# 3. More Will Be Given

*For whosoever hath, to him shall be given, and he shall have more abundance: but whosoever hath not, from him shall be taken away even that he hath.*

Matthew 13:12, King James Version

Imagine if a country tried to have an economy while encouraging everyone to keep their money under the bed.

Absurd! In a short time, no one would have any money at all. They'd spend it, each alone, then it would be gone.

The function of currency is exchange and investment. The function of love is the same.

You think you're sitting on love like a chicken on her eggs. At the same time, you think you're better than other people - at least some of them.

How silly! True love expands infinitely and includes everyone.

# 4. The Coins

*Either what woman having ten pieces of silver, if she lose one piece, doth not light a candle, and sweep the house, and seek diligently till she find it?*

Luke 15:8, King James Version

The Kingdom of God is like a woman on a fixed income, who misplaced her purse. (She absent-mindedly placed it in a corner while going through her mail.)

When she realized it was missing and started retracing her steps, she thought of all the things she'd need to do – contact her credit card company, replace her licenses, and, of course, buy a new purse. How much time and money all this will cost!

She also had $50 in the purse. She eventually found it, and was overcome with relief. To celebrate, she took a friend out to lunch with the $50. She'd been feeling pinched before she thought she lost her purse, but now she's feeling rich!

# 5. The Mustard Seed

*It is like a grain of mustard seed, which a man took, and cast into his garden; and it grew, and waxed a great tree; and the fowls of the air lodged in the branches of it.*

Luke 13:19, King James Version

You think your attitude doesn't matter much, so you're prone to anger. You think the world changes when you get your message out. But if you're fighting fire with fire, you're not promoting change, but more of the same.

It's fine to be an advocate, but advocacy isn't love - it's advocacy. Your intention is good, but if you're acting out of anger, you're not being loving.

You say, "comfort the afflicted and afflict the comfortable!"

But I say, "comfort the afflicted and take care not to afflict anyone else."

Don't turn the wheel of affliction.

Is your intention to stand up for the victims of oppression? Your intention is good, but remember: when we hold anger in our hearts, the downtrodden of today become tomorrow's oppressors.

Love grows like a seed and it grows quietly, out of sight.

The Kingdom of God is like a woman who put a little birdseed out for the chickadees, and one morning she noticed that her yard was full of sunflowers.

Just allow the seed of love to grow in your heart, and all things will be made new again.

# 6. The Light of the World

*Ye are the light of the world.*

Matthew 5:15, King James Version

You are infinite love, so you certainly don't have to attain infinite love. A misunderstanding sometimes arises, and you think, "I need do nothing to attain infinite love. Because I need do nothing, I'd better figure out what "nothing" is, and do it!"

Meditation consists of sitting and breathing, so it looks like doing nothing. (From the outside, anyway!) Meditation then becomes the spiritual practice of choice.

Everything is a perfect, spontaneous manifestation of God,

or Love. All your apparent doing and non-doing are perfect. This is what's meant by, "you need do nothing."

You are the Light of the world.

If light grew dark, what would you light it with?

You are the salt of the earth.

If salt lost its saltiness, how would you salt it?

You concern yourself with seeing, knowing and finding, but it's impossible to be blind, ignorant or lost.

You need do nothing, but until you accept the infinite love that's in you and all around you, "nothing" is the hardest thing to do!

# 7. As Little Children

*Verily I say unto you, Except ye be converted, and become as little children, ye shall not enter into the kingdom of heaven.*

Matthew 18:3, King James Version

Imagine a baby is brought to a lecture hall where a great spiritual master is teaching. If the baby starts fussing, will the master calm him with the power of her presence? Maybe, but if she's truly a great master, she will silence *herself* for the baby.

There's no greater spiritual teacher than a baby. We should bow in reverence to any baby we see, including the baby who still lives in us!

All this time, you've been trying to discipline yourself so you can become gentle and wise. There's a grownup inside you who's been goading the baby inside you to grow up. Imagine your surprise when you see that your inner baby is your true Self, the one you've been searching for!

No professional grownups are enlightened. It's not that the enlightened aren't professionals. They are, but they're professional babies.

Enlightenment is all about innocence.

Everyone is called to infinite love and joy, but you can't get there with your self-image intact. In this sense, the gate *is* narrow. It would

be harder to pull a camel through a
needle's eye than to pull you into
heaven with your self-image intact.

I understand - you want to be
responsible, competent and good.
It doesn't seem like you're
asking for much, but these
qualities imply their opposites.
When you live like this, you spend
your life outrunning your
imperfections. Not so fast!

Just let yourself be as innocent as
a baby, and you'll know that
heaven is already here.

# 8. Rest Easy

*Blessed are the poor in spirit: for theirs is the kingdom of heaven.*

*Blessed are they that mourn: for they shall be comforted.*

Matthew 5:3-4, King James Version

If you are poor, rest easy. Infinite wealth is already inside you.

Give smiles and kind words to your loved ones - love is the wealth that can only increase.

If you are mourning the loss of a loved one, rest easy.

Infinite love is already inside you. People come in and out of our lives for profound reasons we don't control or understand. In our grief, we fall even more deeply in love with the one we mourn. This is a natural and beautiful thing.

Don't feel you didn't love them enough while they were here. You loved them more than you know, and the love you feel now counts just as much.

God has saved every loving thought you've ever had, and all the petty arguments have vanished like the frost.

If you worry about your level of achievement, rest easy.

Infinite power is already yours. Since your only job in this world is to give and receive love, you are always in the perfect position.

If God is for you, who can be against you? All situations are for your infinite good.

You say, "I believe in human goodness. The troublemakers of this world are few and far between, and people are basically kind. If I asked a stranger for help, they'd probably lend a hand. I guess anyone who isn't against me is for me."

But I say: "Even those who appear to be against you are for you, as everything is for your infinite good. Bless even those who appear to oppose you - they are angels in disguise."

# 9. Give

*Give, and it shall be given unto you
(...)*

Luke 6:38, King James Version

Give to everyone who asks. Do you think it's an accident they ran into you and you ran into them? I tell you, they are angels in disguise.

Do you think they will squander your money? Give a dollar, then. You have a hundred times more money than they do, yet you cling to your bank account like a life raft on a tossing sea.

Your only work in this world is to love, but you forgot that the moment you arrived, and you started doing almost everything else. Now *you're* going to complain about *someone else's behavior*? There must be something in the water here.

If you feel pinched, just give a smile or a moment of your attention. Make the person in question feel validated and worthy, even if you think you can't give to them or their cause.

If you feel resentful, just notice your mind. You've thrown the judgement machine into the "on" position. Are any of your assumptions really true of this person or cause?

I find it helpful to think that everyone else is already enlightened, and they're doing what they're doing to help me wake up.

They're all God's angels in disguise
and, as usual, I'm the last to know.

# 10. Love

*(...)Thou shalt love thy neighbour as thyself.*

Mark 12:31, King James Version

Love everyone who approaches, even your apparent adversaries. Love in all directions, and when you pray, focus on Love.

What's the alternative?

If you concern yourself with ambition and attainment, you might get a promotion, a vacation home, and a Lexus. But you might miss the ever-present opportunity of infinite joy - compared to which your "happiness" is but the purest distillation of suffering.

So, stay as innocent as a child and the universe will take care of you.

# 11. The Flowers

*And why take ye thought for raiment? Consider the lilies of the field, how they grow; they toil not, neither do they spin* (...)

Matthew 6:28, King James Version

Don't fret about this so-called life, and the universe will bring you everything you need.

Think of it this way:

Daisies don't get spa therapy, but haven't you heard the expression, "fresh as a daisy?"

Larks don't attend seminars on workplace stress, but haven't you heard the expression, "happy as a lark?"

Infinite joy is your birthright, but you can't receive it if your hands are full.

## 12. Ask

*Ask, and it shall be given you;*
*seek, and ye shall find; knock, and*
*it shall be opened unto you* (...)

Matthew 7:7, King James Version

Love is all around you, and you can
have it if you let it in.

Love doesn't take time to reach
you. Once you realize you want it,
it's yours.

Once you know the path, you've
attained the goal.

Spiritual seekers are seeking the
day after which nothing was ever
the same again. I tell you, that day
is today.

# 13. The Laborers

*These last have wrought but one hour, and thou hast made them equal unto us, which have borne the burden and heat of the day.*

Matthew 20:12, King James Version

You don't need to work for infinite love. It doesn't matter who you think you are or what you think you've done.

You're like a construction worker who got to a work site late. Construction had started months ago, and the house was about to be sold, but you got the same compensation as workers who were on the job when the land was leveled and the foundation poured.

Yes, it's completely unfair. But remember, the basis of this dream is that you don't deserve love. It's always going to feel a little unnerving to open your arms and receive.

# 14. The Prodigal Son

*And he arose, and came to his
father. But when he was yet a
great way off, his father saw him,
and had compassion, and ran, and
fell on his neck, and kissed him.*

Matthew 15:20, King James Version

God loves you infinitely, don't you
know? Hasn't God summoned all
this so you can come home?

You think this world represents the
absence of God's love.

But I tell you, wherever you go,
God is there.

God is the mustard seed in your
soil and the leaven in your bread.

God transforms your hiding place into the Kingdom of God.

You went to the ends of the earth to hide from God's love. You closed your blinds, locked your doors, and planted thick hedges. Then, you climbed into bed and pulled the covers over your head.

You think you don't deserve love. You think you should prove your worth, so you invented a world of dragons to slay and innocents to rescue.

How silly! In reality, you are always home with God.

Only your guilt separates you from God's love. You're like the prodigal son: you squandered your inheritance and lived in hunger and filth. Then, you remembered you're the son of wealth. You returned as a wretched failure, asking to be treated as the lowest servant. Instead, you were embraced as a beloved son.

We are all the prodigal son, thinking we don't deserve infinite love. We made wrong choices and we squandered the wealth of the spirit.

But I tell you, you can't act against God's will, so your every choice piloted your journey home by the shortest route.

You think you've made wrong choices, but that would be impossible. And we all return as wretched failures because there was never anything to be done.

There is a righteous brother in the story who thinks he made good choices and never left God's side. He's jealous of his brother's return to the full embrace of Love.

I tell you, even this brother is the prodigal son, because he doesn't understand that Love is already his.

Your sense of separation from God is based on guilt. Occasionally, you manage to deny your guilt and think you did everything right. Most things, anyway.

In your denial, you make a fearful idol of God and believe God will love you only if you do the right things. In your denial, you've excluded yourself from Love as surely as when you feel guilty and ashamed.

You don't have to swing, like a pendulum, between feeling self-righteous and feeling guilty and ashamed.

Both you and your brother are innocent. And there is nothing you can do to earn Love - Love is already here.

# 15. Magic

*Judge not, that ye be not judged.*

Matthew 7:1

The world is your mirror: if you judge others, you will see others as judging you. If you withhold from others, you will see others as withholding from you.

The magic spell for conquering this mirror-world is to forgive with your whole heart what was never done to you in the first place. (The problem was never out there.)

There is nothing about this that can't be done in an instant.

Forgive completely, like it never happened. Be as kind as you can, and more. Don't dwell on the apparent faults of others.

The world is your mirror, so what can you lose?

# 16. All Healing is Spiritual

*When the unclean spirit is gone out of a man, he walketh through dry places, seeking rest; and finding none, he saith, I will return unto my house whence I came out.*

Luke 11:24, King James Version

You are the Beloved; you are Love itself, and you are the love that joins them together. If someone thinks you're something else, they're mistaken. Knowing your true identity is your best protection.

I know the temptation to focus on ways you think you've been victimized, but where do I begin?

First, this position depends on a false identification with a "self" that can be hurt. You are not this "self." You are Love itself.

Second, you invented all this when you thought, for a second, that you don't deserve infinite love. The instant you had this thought, its "world" was created.

This world is nothing other than the thought: "I don't deserve love." Clearly, this world is going to be a bit bizarre. Why focus on the symptoms?

Third, infinite love immediately transformed your delusion of unlove into a therapy center to help you, and all the troublemakers you populated your world with were immediately transformed into angels in disguise.

Fourth, the position of victimization makes you feel smart and insightful - a bit special, really - like a light unto a darkened world. If you see yourself as a source of wisdom in an ignorant world, you'll wander like a banshee through waterless lands, carrying your lamp of darkness.

That's not what I want for you. Besides, the opposite is true: your apparent self is the only pinpoint of darkness is a world of all-encompassing light.

# 17. The Wisest Course

*Agree with thine adversary quickly, whiles thou art in the way with him; lest at any time the adversary deliver thee to the judge, and the judge deliver thee to the officer, and thou be cast into prison.*

Matthew 5:25, King James Version

Your world is nothing but the spontaneous manifestation of divine perfection. You thought it was something else for a second. Look again.

Do you want a successful life?

I'm not against it, but if only you could see the cosmic joke! This life is as close to death as you're ever going to get.

Don't misunderstand me - dying in an apparent, biological way won't do you any good - you'll just start the program again after a brief intermission.

This program of conflict and lack of love is itself the problem. It covers your vision and it's blocking your view of the Kingdom.

The Kingdom of God is like a financial adviser. His client lost money in a high-risk investment and he's taking the adviser to court. But the adviser has proof that he acted competently: his records show he advised lower risk, diversified investments every step of the way.

The adviser knows he'll win the case, and he imagines his client will get a sharp rebuke from the judge for maligning his reputation and wasting his time.

On his way to court, the adviser realizes the case will become public record. Win or lose, his clients' trust will be affected. He immediately calls the dissatisfied client, apologizes, and arranges to compensate him for part of his losses.

This wise adviser knows: even if he wins in court, he loses if he's *taken* to court. He apologizes and makes amends regardless of who is right.

When your program of conflict is running, even when you win, you lose. When you shut it down you always win, even if you lose.

# 18. Forgive

*So he called every one of his lord's debtors unto him, and said unto the first, How much owest thou unto my lord? And he said, An hundred measures of oil. And he said unto him, Take thy bill, and sit down quickly, and write fifty.*

Luke 16:5-6, King James Version

The Kingdom of God is like a wise couple who own a bakery near a bridge. The bakery did well over the years and the couple loaned money to friends. Now the town is repairing the bridge and their part of town is closed to pedestrians. The construction will be done in six months, but they have two kids in college and they're worried about tuition.

The couple thinks things over carefully:

"We're in a tough place. We'll get some compensation from the town, but we need another source of income now. We'll pay it back easily in a year or two."

They have an insight:

"Many of our friends owe us money. Let's go to them and explain our situation. We'll ask everyone to give us what they can - even if it's a small amount - and we'll cancel their debts completely. If someone can't give us money but can help in some other way, we'll take it with gratitude and cancel their debt."

The wise couple follow their plan. Instead of losing their friends' goodwill by demanding full payment of their debts, goodwill increases exponentially by their forward-thinking kindness.

The Kingdom of God is found when we drop the debt of the past and open ourselves to the love that is all around us, here and now.

# 19. All Around You

*The kingdom of God is all around you, but you don't see it.*

The Gospel of Thomas

You say, "I'll use my spirituality to manifest my best life, now!"

But I say, "infinite love is here in your presence, but you don't see it."

If you would stop worrying about your so-called life, you would discover your life.

If you see yourself as a thoughtful person in a world of incompetence, or a righteous person in a world of corruption, or an enlightened

person in a world of ignorance,
you'll stay asleep, my friend!

# 20. Salvation

*For whosoever will save his life*
*shall lose it: and whosoever will*
*lose his life (…) shall* [save] *it.*

Matthew 16:25, King James Version

Do you want to save the world?
I don't think it can be done.

Everything is a manifestation of
divine perfection, and everyone is
an angel in disguise.

Why doesn't the truth break
through to you? If such love is all
around you, why doesn't it crash
into you with the force of a
thousand suns?

You don't believe it, I guess. You feel too guilty. "What about the suffering in the world?" you think.

You put the cart in front of the horse, my friend!

From time to time, an innocent thought occurs to you: "I don't deserve infinite love." With this thought, you appear to step out of Love for a moment, as if to breathe the ghastly air of nonlove.

Everything that seems to happen afterward is just the exploratory outworking of this thought.

"I don't think I like this," you decide.

You can return to infinite love by snapping your fingers because you never really left. But you think you should resolve the world's suffering – in some way save the world – first. It's understandable given your set of assumptions. Do you see the circle you're in?

You're in this apparent world of nonlove because you feel guilty, and you stay here and suffer out of guilt. Guilt is the launching pad and the landing place of suffering and fear.

You can't do anything from this starting point and you can't help anyone, either. The moment you let go of guilt, you'll be able to help millions. But then you will know that no one needs your help.

You see, we're either enlightened together, or we're together in darkness.

If you can't see the light that's already here, you will stumble in darkness, even if you think you're leading the way. (The fact that you think there are ignorant people to lead is a symptom that you're lost.)

Just remember the Love you once knew. The light of Love travels effortlessly on the road of thought because once you remember it, it's here.

You certainly tried to live outside Love. You built an ornate sand castle, and you were anxious every moment that the wind would topple its towers.

You thought it might shelter you, but you couldn't really trust it as it was made of sand.

One day, the tide took it.

*Selah*. You can see the sunrise now.

Printed in Great Britain
by Amazon

42632263R00047